Credit Repair & the 30 Day Transformation

A Comprehensive Guide to Removing Negative Marks & Increasing Your Credit Score

Introduction

Imagine your entire life's credit performance reduced to a three digit number. You do not have to imagine it because it is real and chances are right at this moment, three credit agencies are now adding all your balances in your credit cards, computing all your unpaid mortgages and counting all days of delayed payments.

 Now, you may think that these agencies with their sophisticated software and complex algorithms generate an accurate report of your credit life. The truth is far from that, various studies show than anything from 1 to 4 in 5 reports are erroneous.

This is why credit repair is a vital necessity for your financial reputation. Banks, creditors and other financial institutions usually start assessing your application for loans using your credit score. In turn, the score is generated by your credit report. The report is generated by your creditors.

Somewhere along the way from the moment your creditor provides the data to the agency, something can go wrong. One wrong figure in your social security number, a delay in updating your credit card statement or a missing mortgage account can wreak havoc in your credit score.

This book will guide you in not only spotting those errors but also correcting them. On top of that, tips and tricks on how to remove seemingly permanent negative records are also included. Finally, strategies on how to make sound financial decisions that can increase your score are also discussed in detail.

information is without contract or any type of guarantee assurance.

Table of Contents

Introduction

Chapter One: Understanding Your Credit Report

Chapter Two: Understanding Your Credit Score & Meaning

Chapter Three: Where to Get Free or Paid Credit Reports?

Chapter Four: How to Check Your Credit Report for Errors?

Chapter Five: Pros & Cons of Credit Repair Services

Chapter Six: 22 Ways to Increase Your Credit Report

Chapter Seven: How to Remove Negative Marks from Your Credit Report?

Chapter Eight: FAQ & Sample Letters

Conclusion

Chapter One: Understanding Your Credit Report

Your credit report is the single most important document for your financial life. The report may seem relatively trivial to you as it only contains information that you may already know personal data, credit history and accounts. However, for other, especially your potential creditors, each entry can mean the approval or disapproval of your loan application.

The compilation of this information is made possible because of the credit bureau. Take note, while you may have a mortgage account in Bank A, a credit card in Bank B or a loan in Lending Institution C, all these information from each of your respective banks and financial institutions are stored in a credit bureau. This is made possible because every time you fill out a form applying for a credit card, a loan or any instrument for credit, the form is sent to the bureau. Your personal data is used to match the application form with any other form or information that is already in file in the bureau.

The credit report is also called credit history or credit score in other countries but they all contain the same type of information. Regardless of what it is called, it is essentially your financial reputation. You may think that such personal or private information remain confidential and known only to you and to your banks. However, the credit report has another purpose aside as a documentation of all your financial information.

Whenever you apply for another credit instrument, for example a credit card or a loan, the bank or financing institution will request your credit report from the credit bureau. They will use the report as a tool to evaluate your qualification for your application. For example, they can measure if you are a good payer of debt if you are always on time on your payments.

You may be overwhelmed on the information, words, dates, figures and numbers on your credit report. There are generally four categories from which all information in the credit report belongs. These are:

1. Personal information and it contains:
   a. Your name and other aliases that you may have used
   b. Your current and previous addresses
   c. Your date of birth
   d. Your social security number
   e. Your current and previous employment

2. Public information and it contains:
   a. Liens
   b. Judgments
   c. Bankruptcies
   d. Wage garnishments
   e. Other open legal issues that have yet to be resolved

3. Creditor information and it contains:
   a. Accounts, whether closed, open or current or charged off
   b. Ownership of the account, whether individual or joint
   c. The balance of the loan

d. The last payment made on the loan

e. Terms of the loan

f. Credit limit

g. Adverse account information and it contains information about loans with which you have late payments, remaining balance and any other account that has been forwarded to a collection agency. The information in this category generally hurt your credit reputation.

h. Any other information pertaining to your payment performance

4. Credit inquiries and it contains:

a. Hard inquiries, these are made by lenders who requested for your credit report to assess any application you may have made. The name of the bank, address, and phone number will be listed as an inquirer. Usually, if you have applied for a loan for example, the name of the bank or financial institution will appear in this section.

b. Soft inquiries, these are made either by you or pre-approved products made by marketing agencies of credit card companies and other lenders.

Chapter Two: Understanding Your Credit Score & Meaning

A credit score is a number that mirrors your entire credit portfolio, performance and discipline in a specific time frame. It is primarily meant for lenders who evaluate loan applications. Before, it took lenders weeks or months to determine your capacity to pay loan and grant your application. Sometimes, you end up getting disqualified. With credit scores, lenders become faster, more efficient and most importantly adjust their loan offer to you based on your score.

An example of a credit score is the FICO score in the United States. The Fair Isaac Corporation has been using math and other statistics to determine the US citizens' credit score since 1956. Through the FICO score, both client and lenders enjoy an efficient, unbiased and safe lending environment.

Credit scores are usually three digit figures starting from 300 to 850. The higher the score is the better is your credit performance. Below is the scale with their corresponding rating:

1.   300 to 550, poor credit

2.   550 to 620, subprime credit

3.   620 to 680, acceptable credit

4.   680 to 740, good credit

5.   740 to 850, excellent credit

Less than 2% of the population has 499 scores, 5% have 549 scores, 8% have 599 scores, 12% have 649 scores and 15% have 650 to 699 scores. The bulk of the population has 749 scores with 18%, 799 scores with 27% and 850 scores with 13%. This shows that the scores are approximately half of the population belong to the lower scores and the other half on the higher scores.

Aside from the population, age also shows a pattern in the credits score. Most 18 to 24 year olds have 638, 25 to 34 with 652, 35 to 44 with 659, 45 to 54 with 685 and 55 and above have 724.

It is difficult or almost impossible to recommend a good credit score. This is because banks and lending institutions are more than willing to serve even those with low credit scores. The only but important difference between those with high and low scores is the interest rate. As a rule, the lower your score is, the higher your interest rate will be. The higher your score is, the lower the interest rate. This rule is applicable to major loan instruments, such as housing and car loans and credit cards.

For example, if you apply for a standard $160,000 mortgage in a 30 year term, the lender will offer you around 9.5% interest rate if you have a poor credit score. This amounts to $259,000 in total payments. On the other hand, if you have an excellent credit score, your interest rate will be offered at around 3.9%. Your total interest payment will be around $89,000.

If you apply for a standard car loan of $25,000 in a 5 year term, the lender will offer you 18.9% or around $13,000 in interest payments if you have a poor credit score. If you have an excellent credit score, your interest rate will be at 5.1% or around $3,500 total interest payments.

This shows how important credit scores are in your financial transactions. They could mean hundreds of thousands of dollars in difference and savings. It is equally important to manage your scores well and especially if you plan to apply for a new loan. Some banks and financial institutions, depending on their risk appetite, may be willing to approve your loan at your expense, in the form of higher interest. Other companies may even offer you pre-approved loans with low interest rates because of your excellent scores.

If you have a poor credit score, there is a huge probability that you will be denied in all your loan applications. Only bankrupt individuals and those with more than 75% delinquency rates belong to this category.

If you have a subprime score, there is a small chance that your loan applications will be granted. However, the terms will really be unfavorable to you. Expect high interest and penalty rates. It is best to postpone the application until you improve your score.

If you have an acceptable score, you will have better chances on your application. However, it will still not be on the best rates.   Only few individuals with good scores are denied on their application.

It is almost a guarantee that your loan will be granted in this score. You are a guaranteed a loan and best interest rates if you have an excellent credit score. Take note that just by reaching the minimum 740 threshold, you are part of the excellent score category and you can already enjoy the privileges of those with 741 or extra points in their credit score.

However, it is also best to try to aim for higher scores beyond 741. This is because the extra points may be used as a buffer in case your credit reports become unfavorable. When the reports lower your credit score, the decrease will not be as much because you have points in reserve.

Note that the score may be standard but lenders will have their own criteria for granting a loan. You may have a high score but a lender may disapprove you because of other factors outside your credit score. For example, banks always factor in not only your credit but also your income.

The credit score is calculated based on your portfolio of loans and your performance on paying these loans. Each criterion does not have equal value or each has its own weight in the final credit score. There are generally five categories that form the computation of your credit score:

1. Payment history

2. Principal amount

3. Loan term or length

4. Credit types

5. New credit

Payment history, this has the largest weight in your credit score. It amounts to 35% of the total. This criterion depends on your payment of your loans. The more you pay on time, the better the score will be. Take note that if you have made one or two late payments, these instances do not automatically reduce your score in this category. Most of the time, few late instances are negligible compared to the overall payment history. The more punctual you are on payment, the higher the score is.

Principal amount, this has the second largest weight in your credit score. It amounts to 30% of the total. This score depends on how close you are to reaching the credit limit of your account. Often called maxing out, for example the balance of your credit card is only a few dollars shy from its maximum credit limit. The closer you are to the limit, the lower the score is.

Loan term, this criterion amounts to 15% of the total credit score. This refers to the length of time that you have held the account. For example, you have been subscribing to the credit card account for more than 5 years or you have been paying your monthly installments for a 10 year long term loan. The longer you have an active account, the higher the score is.

Credit types amount to 10% of the total credit score. This refers to the portfolio of accounts that you have. For example, you may have several credit cards, loans for various purposes, mortgages and retail accounts. You may have these accounts in either a bank or a financial institution. The more diverse your portfolio is, the higher the score is.

New credit amounts to 10% of the total credit score. This refers to any pending application or inquiries you have made for new loans. The more inquiries you have, the lower the score is.

Chapter Three: Where to Get Free or Paid Credit Reports?

First and foremost before you can even begin to check for the accuracy of your credit report, you need to get a hold of the report. There are three credit reporting agencies in the United States. These are Experian, TransUnion and Equifax. Since 2005, each person can receive one free report per year from these agencies.

You only need to request for your report to the Annual Credit Report, which is the sole authorized agency to process free reports. You can actually get one report from each of the three agencies, which means you can get three per year. Furthermore, you are also entitled to free reports if a bank or financial institution denies your application.

It is important that you are able to get not just one report, it would be best if you can get a hold of all three. This is because each agency will have their format and there will be subtle differences between reports. Another reason is that one agency may not be able to capture your account on one institution but the other will. Also, the same information may be available on one agency but will be stored in different sections or headings of the report.

Below is the Annual Credit Report Request Form that you can use to claim your free credit report. You may click on the picture to bring you to the actual site to download the form.

Annual Credit Report Request Form

You have the right to get a free copy of your credit file disclosure, commonly called a credit report, once every 12 months, from each of the nationwide consumer credit reporting companies - Equifax, Experian and TransUnion.

For instant access to your free credit report, visit www.annualcreditreport.com.

For more information on obtaining your free credit report, visit www.annualcreditreport.com or call 877-322-8228.

Use this form if you prefer to write to request your credit report from any, or all, of the nationwide consumer credit reporting companies. The following information is required to process your request. Omission of any information may delay your request.

Once complete, fold (do not staple or tape), place into a #10 envelope, affix required postage and mail to:

Annual Credit Report Request Service P.O. Box 105281 Atlanta, GA 30348-5281.

Please use a Black or Blue Pen and write your responses in PRINTED CAPITAL LETTERS without touching the sides of the boxes like the examples listed below:

| A | B | C | D | E | F | G | H | I | J | K | L | M | N | O | P | Q | R | S | T | U | V | W | X | Y | Z | 0 | 1 | 2 | 3 | 4 | 5 | 6 | 7 | 8 | 9 |

Social Security Number:

[ ][ ][ ] - [ ][ ] - [ ][ ][ ][ ]

Date of Birth:

[ ][ ] / [ ][ ] / [ ][ ][ ][ ]
Month / Day / Year

— Fold Here —   — Fold Here —

First Name / M.I.

Last Name / JR, SR, III, etc.

Current Mailing Address:

House Number / **Street Name**

Apartment Number / Private Mailbox / **For Puerto Rico Only: Print Urbanization Name**

City / **State** / **ZipCode**

Previous Mailing Address (complete only if at current mailing address for less than two years):

House Number / **Street Name**

— Fold Here —   — Fold Here —

Apartment Number / Private Mailbox / **For Puerto Rico Only: Print Urbanization Name**

City / **State** / **ZipCode**

Shade Circle Like This → ●
Not Like This → ⊠ ☑

I want a credit report from (shade each that you would like to receive):
○ Equifax
○ Experian
○ TransUnion

○ Shade here if, for security reasons, you want your credit report to include no more than the last four digits of your Social Security Number.

In case you want to view your credit report more than once from one credit agency or on another report from the same agency but on a different year, you can still do so. However, it will come at a cost. Experian will charge you a membership fee of $21.95 per month but it will allow you to order a $1 credit report trial membership. TransUnion has the same trial offer but a membership fee of $17.95. Equifax offers it for $15.95 and a complete report from the remaining two agencies for $39.95.

Chapter Four: How to Check Your Credit Report for Errors?

Credit reports as powerful as they may be are unfortunately not foolproof. Credit reports can suffer from errors which will hurt your credit reputation. However financially responsible you are, your discipline may not be properly reflected on your credit report. This is why it is important to be vigilant on your credit report.

Statistics show that anywhere from 1 to 4 out every 5 credit reports have errors. Out of those statistics, 5% were denied applications because of erroneous reporting. 10% of those who discovered the errors were able to adjust their scores by more than 50 points. While the credit agencies are responsible for generating the report, you are responsible for the accuracy of the report itself.

A telltale sign that there is an error in your report is by comparing all three reports for the agencies. If your credit score is noticeably different or has a large discrepancy from one report to another, then this means that one, two or all three are missing data which the other agency has.

There are generally three sources of errors in your credit report:

1. Data sources

2. Time lapses

3. Fraud

4. Time delays

5. Persona information

Most errors do not come from the credit agency itself but the sources of their data. For example, your bank may have overlooked sending an updated status of your credit card account. Even though you have paid the amount in full, in your credit report, an outstanding balance still exists.

Another error is one time lapses. Take note that any history of bad debts, whether paid or unpaid, will appear within 7 years. Bankruptcy will be listed in your report for 10 years. Make sure that you count the years since you have failed to pay the debt. If your bad debt is still listed after 7 years, then that is a credit report error.

Identity theft is rampant with the various modus operandi for stealing credit card information. If you fail to notice unauthorized transactions on your bank statement, then any unpaid transactions will still be included in your credit report.

Also each of the credit agencies has their own cut off periods in generating their report. It may not be a matter of erroneous reporting but only of delayed reporting. One agency may have generated a report on your most recent payment while the other agency will report on the next period.

There will also be errors if you have been using different names, such as aliases, in your financial transactions. This will result to a credit report that is fragmented, with one set of data found on your real name and the other on another name. Other discrepancies may also be a result of varying personal information such as inaccuracies in social security numbers, addresses or a change of last name for newly married women.

Any dispute you make must be well-documented. For example, if you have fully paid a loan but the report says you still have an outstanding balance, you need to provide a copy of the receipt of full payment. Any communication you make with your bank or financial institution must be put in writing and then the credit agency must be furnished a copy of your letter.

If you are sending by postal service or by email, request a return receipt or a notification that the letter has been received. Include the confirmation of receipt in your documents for dispute. Usually, the credit agency is given 30 days to investigate and verify your dispute. In turn, the creditor is given another 30 days to either confirm or reject your dispute.

 If the creditor does not respond within 30 days of the agency's notification, then the entry must be deleted. If there is any delay in your dispute, you may ask the credit agency to include your statement of dispute on your credit report. Although it is your responsibility to verify your credit report, it is the credit agency that is responsible for correcting it.

When you write a dispute, it is best to provide all information. Identify exactly the specifics of your dispute, the item, the amount, the status or any detail that is erroneous. Next, state the facts and your position on the dispute. Finally, you need to request for changes in the credit report either by correcting or deleting the figures. Write professionally and avoid any negative, threatening or emotionally laden remarks.

Here is a sample of a dispute letter:

[Your Name]
[Your Address]
[Your City, State, Zip Code]

[Date]

Complaint Department
[Company Name]
[Street Address]
[City, State, Zip Code]

Dear Sir or Madam:

I am writing to dispute the following information in my file. I have circled the items I dispute on the attached copy of the report I received.

This item [identify item(s) disputed by name of source, such as creditors or tax court, and identify type of item, such as credit account, judgment, etc.] is [inaccurate or incomplete] because[describe what is inaccurate or incomplete and why]. I am requesting that the item be removed [or request another specific change] to correct the information.

Enclosed are copies of [use this sentence if applicable and describe any enclosed documentation, such as payment records and court documents] supporting my position. Please reinvestigate this[these] matter[s] and [delete or correct] the disputed item[s] as soon as possible.

Sincerely,

Your name
Enclosures: [List what you are enclosing.]

This letter can be found at:
http://www.consumer.ftc.gov/articles/0384-sample-letter-disputing-errors-your-credit-report

When you have an accurate credit report that is reflective of your true credit standing, then you can enjoy the benefits of your financial discipline.

Your credit report is your credit reputation. The better it is, the easier your financial life will be. For example, you can get approval of your loan faster just by your score. While before it took banks or financial institutions weeds or even months to evaluate your loan application, today with credit scores they have an instant measurement for your capacity to pay and financial discipline.

Also the credit report makes processing of your loans fairer, it can remove bias based on gender, race, religion, marital status and other personal information. Most lenders have the tendency to evaluate you beyond your financial capacity. With a credit report, they can focus only on what is essential in qualifying you for a loan. Past credit history may be corrected as you improve your financial responsibility. This was once impossible when a bad debt becomes a permanent fixture in your records.

More loans are also made possible because lenders can offer you a wide range of products that matches your score. Instead of a few standard products that may disqualify you in your application, lenders can adjust their offer based on your score, instead of denying you altogether. With credit reports, lenders are able to reduce the cost of their credit investigation activities. In turn, they are able to offer lower interest rates. For example, the United States enjoys lower interest rates compared to European countries because of the availability of credit reports.

Chapter Five: Pros & Cons of Credit Repair Services

Once you have cleared your credit report from any errors and the score it is still not up to par to what you want, then you may require the services of credit repair agencies. These agencies have experience in cleaning up your history, delinquencies, charge offs and other negative information in your report. They will make also make disputes on your behalf.

Most of these credit repair agencies work on loopholes in the rules that determine your report and score. For example, if the agency did not verify or used improper means to verify the data they received from their source, then it can be a cause for dispute. The credit bureau usually uses automated software to make the verification but actual calls are still required. If they cannot provide proof of the call, then it can be a cause for dispute.

Legitimate credit repair agencies do not claim that by employing them, they will guarantee a significant increase in your credit score. These services only work if you actually have errors in your report that you cannot verify or resolve on your own. The main activity of these agencies is to check for inaccuracies in your report which in turn increases your score. This means that their repair services come with both advantages and disadvantages.

Pros

Years of experience, this is the single most important benefit that you can receive from their services. Most individuals may not have enough workable knowledge that can be applied in the repair of their own credit report and score. However, these agencies know the entire system behind the reporting and the scoring. They will know loopholes and techniques that will work on your favor. In fact, they can even identify errors that when made by the credit agency, can be penalized. For example, you are to receive $1000 in damages if a 7 year old negative item is still listed.

Network with creditors, most of these credit repair service agencies already have long term relationships with creditors themselves. This means they can take advantage of any considerations or legitimate exceptions that can be done on your behalf.

Personalized service, since your credit history, performance and report are unique to you, hiring them will offer you a customized service and solution that are fit to your needs. They can take into consideration the other aspects of your financial background, such as income and expense streams, to guide you on making the right decisions for your credit report.

Cons

Cost, this is the main disadvantage of these agencies. Most people who are seeking these services already have problems in their finances. The added expense of the agency's fees may only hurt their finances. However, for some people the benefits that the service provides far outweigh the cost. These agencies also offer money back guarantee in case you are unsatisfied.

Upfront payment, aside from monthly payments, some agencies require an initial payment even before any work is done on your credit report. Some of the amounts are more than $100. It is best that you do your research on any agency before you employ their services.

No guarantees, no legitimate agency can promise that they will be able to increase your scores with their intervention. Since the work usually requires more months of processing, it will cost you more. You may end up with a small increase in your score after months of disputes and investigations.

Chapter Six: 22 Ways to Increase Your Credit Report

There are several ways to increase your credit score. The secret to raising your score lies in the understanding of the criteria that make up the score itself. If you know how each category raises or lowers your score, then you can make steps to either increase the factors that raise the score or minimize or reduce the factors that lower the score. Remember the five categories and the corresponding weight of the components of your score:

1. Payment history is 35%

2. Principal amount is 30%

3. Loan term or length is 15%

4. Credit types is 10%

5. New credit is 10%

Payment History

1. Make timely payments on your loan. Sometimes it is not a matter of having the money but on remembering the due dates. Request your bank or lender to enroll you in an automated system that reminds you of your due date via text or email. Enroll your other payments on a payment scheme that automatically deducts your debit card.

2. If you have the funds available, it is best if you can pay your monthly installment earlier than the due date. For example, your due date is on the 20th but your credit card reports to the credit agency on the 10th of the month. Even if you pay on your due date, your dated

credit report will still show a balance even if you have paid already.

3. You can also beat the cut off periods by paying more than once on your credit. This way you do not need to have to wait for the report to be generated with high balances when you already have the money to pay for it.

4. If you are late on your payment this month, do not postpone the next payment to the next month. Pay as soon as you can since your credit score counts the length of time you are delayed on your payments. A few late payments will not hurt your overall score but consistent delays will.

Principal Amount

5. Request your bank to increase the limit of your credit card but do not max the card. Remember, the closer you are to the limit, the lower the score is. The converse is also true, the farther you are to the limit, the higher the score is. For example, you have $1000 outstanding balance to a $1,500 maximum limit. This will have a lower score compared to a $1000 outstanding balance to a $3,000 maximum limit, which only has a 1/3 debt to limit ratio. It is recommended that you use only 30% of your credit limit. Usually, a request for a higher credit limit can be justified by prompt payments.

6. When choosing between two credit card payments when you can only pay one, it is best to choose strategically. It is always best to pay the one with the highest balance or the one with the highest interest, however for a quick fix on your credit score, it is best to pay off the credit card with a higher utilization ratio. For example you have an $800 balance on a $1000 limit card and a $1500 balance on a $2000 limit card. The first card has a ratio of 80%. The second card has a ratio of 75%. The first card lowers your score more than the second card, it is best to pay off the first card first.

7. Stop using your credit cards altogether if you are only settling the minimum amount per month. Start paying the credit cards that have the highest interest rates and work down the lower ones. There are cases when withdrawing money from your investment portfolio is a better option that shouldering the outstanding balance on your remaining funds. This is because the returns you may get from your investment may be outweighed by the interest payments you make on your loans.

Loan term or length

8. Do not open new credit or loans. They may increase your loan diversity but it will lower your average account age. For example you have a credit card with Bank A for 5 years and another card with Bank B for 15 years. This gives you an average of 10 years. If you open a new account with Bank C, your account age will drop to 6 years.

9. Keep old credit accounts active. They are proof of your financial responsibility and also increase the average years of credit activity. Removing old accounts will cause your financial age to become younger and therefore riskier. Keep your old accounts, this way your financial age will become older and therefore more experienced.

Credit type

10. If you have unused credit cards, consider keeping rather than cancelling them. This maintains your loan portfolio diversity. However, do not think that adding more credit cards will increase your score. The secret is proportion; it is recommended that for every installment loan you have two revolving loans. For example, if you have a car loan, it is best to have two credit cards.

11. Make sure that your credit report is a laundry list of all of your financial accounts, especially those which you

have a good standing. For example, your old mobile phone subscription you had for more than 10 years, your cable and internet provider, utilities and any other company that receives your monthly payments deserve to be on your report.

New credit

12. Whenever you intend to take a loan, shop for interest rates within a 2 week period. This is because when you take too much time in sending out applications, the number of inquiries will hurt your score. On the other hand, packing together all applications into this time period will only count as one inquiry.

13. Minimize inquiries on your report, the more inquiries made on you report on a short time, for example a year, will reduce your score. For example, if you want a car loan, you can inquire as many times as you want within a 30 to 45 day period. However for soft inquiries that are recurrent, the score will be drop.

14. If you do not have a credit card, this will actually lower your credit score. Having a credit card and managing it properly, via consistent use but timely payments, shows that you have financial responsibility. Furthermore, the activity you get in credit cards, such as payments, will serve to increase your score on the payment history category.

15. If you have not applied for a loan in your life, this will also lower your credit score. This is because the credit bureau will have little information about you in the financial environment and it will consider you as risky. Consider taking a loan with the minimum amount to establish your financial responsibility. This is also true if you have no credit activity for long periods of time.

Other Ways

16. Dispute any errors in your report. Any dispute that is unaddressed by your creditor for more than 30 days will automatically be removed from your report. Filing a dispute is free, start by addressing the major errors such as unpaid balances when you already have them paid. This will create an instant boost to your score. If you are nearing the threshold of the next credit score category, then you can dispute the minor errors since those small points will make the difference.

17. Consider borrowing money from family or friends to increase artificially increase the score because of your payments. If you have gained the trust of your family or friends, ask to be an authorized user or a supplemental owner of their credit card. This way you can take advantage of the already approved credit line that will affect your utilization ratio.

18. If you have children and you want to them to begin building their credit reputation, you can also make them authorized users of your credit accounts. The earlier you start, the older their accounts will be and the higher their financial experience will be in the sight of credit agencies.

19. Any new credit account must appear as soon as possible in your report. This will increase your diversity and also your score.

20. Enroll your credit report to a freeze report scheme. This way in case of a report of fraud, the credit agencies will automatically prevent creditors from accessing your credit report.

21. In case of a divorce, prioritize the settlement of all loans that are jointly owned by the couple. If not possible, amend the loan terms by removing one name in the loan. These steps are necessary because even after the divorce, the credit report will still record any loans on both of your names.

22. Avoid filing for bankruptcy. The short term advantage of filing will be far outweighed by the long term efforts you need to make to restore your financial standing. Bankruptcy drops your score considerably and automatically disqualifies your applications for loans from other companies.

Except for bankruptcy, your credit score does not significantly change in a short period of time. Your score in this month may experience minor or even negligible fluctuations in the next month. Improving your score is not an overnight effort with an overnight result. It usually takes between 6 to 12 months before you can achieve the score that you want.

With this information in mind, it is best that you delay any loan application for at least 6 months while you take steps to improve you score. This is why getting reports whether on a monthly or quarterly basis is important. This will allow you to monitor your progress. The reports can encourage you to push forward if you are on the right course or make changes if you do not get the numbers you want every end of the month.

Chapter Seven: How to Remove Negative Marks from Your Credit Report?

There are also ways to remove any negative marks on your credit report aside from the dispute of legitimate errors. These steps have to do more with the use of negotiation skills and personal relationships. These steps are made possible because while credit agencies are obligated to verify the data they receive, the lenders are not required to report their lending activities to the credit reporting agencies.

1. Request for a goodwill adjustment. This is a more personal approach that you require to make towards your creditors. You may write what is called a goodwill letter. It is essentially a letter seeking for compassion towards removing from your file any past delinquencies. Find the name of your creditor or the one in charge of your accounts; tell him of your reasons behind the late payment. It can be because of a temporary unemployment phase, an unexpected expense because of an illness or accident, a death in the family or any reason that can tug at their emotions. Use the term "goodwill adjustment" instead of "remove" or "delete."

   Here is a sample of a goodwill letter:

   Your Name
   Your Address
   Your City, State Zip

   Date

   Company Name
   Company Address

City, State Zip

Re: Account Number

To Whom It May Concern:
I've enjoyed being a customer of Bank A since 1995.
Today, I'm writing to request a goodwill adjustment to
my credit files.

I was a model customer from the time I received my
credit card in 1995 until 2006, when I suffered a
medical illness which wrecked my finances and my
ability to make timely credit card payments. As a result,
I fell behind on my payments by 60 days. Fortunately, I
was able to turn my financial situation around and I've
been timely with my payments ever since.

I'm preparing to shop for a mortgage and was told
those late payments will keep me from getting the
best interest rate. I'm requesting a goodwill adjustment
since the payments do not reflect my current payment
status. Thank you for your time reading this letter and
the consideration you've given my situation.

Sincerely,

Your Name

This letter can be found at:
http://credit.about.com/od/creditrepair/qt/Sample-

2. Give and take. You can also negotiate with your creditor for an exchange on their removal of your negative records on their next report to the credit agencies. For example, you can offer your creditor to enroll your loan in an automatic payment scheme using your debit card. This way you are showing him that you are committed to pay and you only want your credit report to mirror your improved financial decisions. You can also make other offers such as restricting your loan in such a way that the creditors will have an advantage but in return, they will omit your negative records on their reports.

3. Pay in full. If you have the funds available, you can even make the deal sweeter to your creditor. In exchange for the removal of your negative records, you are willing to pay the entire amount. This is called a pay for delete offer. Make sure to keep it writing and request both a confirmation of receipt of your letter and a signed agreement of your creditor to your offer.

Here is a sample of a pay for delete letter:

Your Name

Your Address

Your City, State Zip

Collector's Name

Collector's Address

Collector's City, State Zip

Date

Re: Account Number XXXX-XXXX-XXXX-XXXX

Dear Collection Manager:

This letter is in response to your [letter / call / credit report entry] on [date] related to the debt referenced above. I wish to save us both some time and effort by settling this debt.
Please be aware that this is not an acknowledgment or acceptance of the debt, as I have not received any verification of the debt. Nor is this a promise to pay and is not a payment agreement unless you provide a response as detailed below.

I am aware that your company has the ability to report this debt to the credit bureaus as you deem necessary. Furthermore, you have the ability to change the listing since you are the information furnisher.

I am willing to pay [this debt in full / $XXX as settlement for this debt] in return for your agreement to remove all information regarding this debt from the credit reporting agencies within ten calendar days of payment. If you agree to the terms, I will send certified payment in the amount of $XXX payable to [Collection Agency] in exchange to have all information related to this debt removed from all of my credit files.

If you accept this offer, you also agree not to discuss the offer with any third-party, excluding the original creditor. If you accept the offer, please prepare a letter on your company letterhead agreeing to the terms. This letter should be signed by an authorized agent of [Collection Agency]. The letter will be treated as a contract and subject to the laws of my state.

As granted by the Fair Debt Collection Practices Act, I have the right to dispute this alleged debt. If I do not receive your postmarked response within 15 days, I will withdraw the offer and request full verification of this debt.

Please forward your agreement to the address listed above.

Sincerely,

Your Name

4. Wait. Time heals all wounds, even financial ones. Take advantage of the 7 year statute of limitation of your negative records or 10 years if you have filed for bankruptcy. Charge offs take seven years and 180 days. Student loans, paid taxes, foreclosures and lawsuits are also dropped after seven years. While waiting, if you make better financial decisions, you can improve on your score as you wait for the seven year period. In fact positive records can average out your negative records that will result to a higher credit score even before the 7 years elapse.

Chapter Eight: FAQ & Sample Letters

Vocabulary of Credit Reports

Your credit report will have terms that are not familiar to an average person. It is best to understand the meaning of each of term so that you are in a better position to evaluate or question the contents of the report. Here are terms that are usually used by credit reporting agencies:

Charged-off

This is a type of status given on delinquent account. This means that the bank or financial institution has failed in its attempts to get you to pay on your debt. It has forwarded your debt to a collections agency for further legal solutions. Even if you have already settled the debt, this status will be on your record for seven years. The seven year period starts from the date when your loan has been constantly unpaid.

Installment account

This is an account type that refers to your standard loans, which you pay in a monthly basis on a fixed rate. It has the standard loan characteristics like a principal amount, an interest rate, a loan term and a monthly payment amount.

Revolving account

This is an account type that refers to your standard credit cards. It does not have a fixed rate of payment and you do not have an obligation to pay it in full every month.

Collection account

This is an account type that refers to all your debts that are already in the hands of a collection agency.

There are also codes that are used in your credit report:

CURR ACCT: Account is in good standing and is current

CUR WAS 30-2: Account is current but was delayed in payment twice for 30 days

PAID: Account is inactive because balance has already been paid

CHARGOFF: This is the shortcut for the charge off status

COLLECT: Account has been sent to collections because of repeated late payments

FORECLOS: Property was foreclosed

BKLIREQ: Debt was forgiven often due to bankruptcy provisions such as Chapter 7, 11 or 13

DELINQ 60: Account is unpaid for 60 days

Dispute Contacts

Send your disputes to the following agencies with their respective addresses and other contact details:

Equifax
 P.O. Box 740256
Atlanta, GA 30374-0241
800-685-1111
www.equifax.com

Experian
P.O. Box 2002
Allen, TX 75013
888-397-3742
www.experian.com

TransUnion
P.O. Box 2000

Chester, PA 19022
800-888-4213
www.transunion.com

List of Reputable Credit Repair Services

Take note that most of these credit service repair agencies offer money-back guarantee for unsatisfied customers.

1. Academy credit. Initial payment of $49.95 to $129 and monthly payments of $9.95 to $69.95
2. Credit Firm. Cost is $39.95 per month.
3. Credit People. 6 months of unlimited services for $316.
4. Credit Repair. Cost is $89.95 per month.
5. Credit Repair Consultant. Initial payment of $189 and monthly payments of $35 to $65.
6. E Credit Attorney. Initial payment of $29 and monthly payments of $29.
7. Lexington Law. Initial payment of $99 and monthly services from $39.95 to $79.95
8. My Credit Group. Initial payment of $99 and monthly payments of $69.
9. National Credit Fixers. Initial payment of $199 and monthly payments of $149.
10. Ovation Credit Report Repair. Offers free consultation, initial payment of $87 and monthly fees of $37 to $57.
11. Sky Blue Credit. Initial and monthly payment of $49.
12. The Credit Pros. Initial payment of $119 to $199 and monthly payments of $50 to $99.
13. Veracity Credit. Initial payment of $69 to $99 and monthly payments of $49 to $79.
14. 180 Credit Solutions and Trinity Credit Services have fees that are quoted on a case to case basis.

Sample Letters

Late Payment
1. Late Payment Dispute
2. Late Payment Explanation

Sample 1: Late Payment Dispute

[Your Name]

[Your Address]

[City, State Zip]

[Credit Bureau]

[Credit Bureau Address]

[City, State Zip]

Date: [DATE]

RE: [Creditor Name and Account number]

This letter is to inform you that the above creditor is reporting me as being late in [MY/OUR] payments and is an error. [MY/OUR]) records show that we have never been late with a payment. [I/WE] have attached a copy of [MY/OUR] records. This reporting error is negatively affecting my credit rating. As you are aware, failure to comply with federal regulations by credit reporting agencies are in serious violation of the Fair Credit Reporting Act and may be investigated by the FTC.

Please correct this error as soon as possible. Please send me notification when it has been corrected since it is negatively affecting my credit.

Thank you for your help,
Sincerely,

[Your Signature]

_____

[Your name typed]

Sample 2: Late Payment Explanation

Re: Mortgage (FHA and/or VA Loan Application)

Dear Sir or Madam:

This letter provides explanations for each derogatory item on my credit report obtained in connection to my mortgage application.

1. Late payments dated 12/07 and 01/08 in regards to current ACME Credit Union (Auto loan) –
balance $845

In December 2007, immediately prior to the loan's "due date" (December 20th) while speaking with an account specialist, I accepted their kind offer to "skip-a-payment" (a yearly offer during the holidays) in order to be more generous with my family during that holiday season. Having been assured that arrangement had been made, I did not send in that month's payment.

January 21, 2008, I remitted my January payment, unaware that a "mix-up" had occurred in processing my "skip-a-payment," causing my January payment to actually be applied to my December 2007 payment. As I unaware of the situation, I did not make the "extra" payment to apply to my January 2008 payment, which would have brought my account current.

I was notified of this situation in February (approximately the 20th) when I arrived at my local branch to make my February payment. I explained the situation and immediately paid the delinquent amount, thus bringing my account current.

As I had believed the matter to be resolved, and being fairly ignorant of FICO scoring, I did not believe there was reason to check my credit reports until March 2008. Whereupon, I realized that the misunderstanding had been reported to the major credit bureaus. I immediately called Tyndall and spoke to the account specialist who then said that it was "too late" to fix, but apologized for her part in the misunderstanding.

2. Late payment dated 04/08 in regards to current ACME Credit Union (Auto loan) – balance $845

This incident was purely a lack of attentiveness on my end. As I was on travel for the US Navy near the due date, I requested that my wife mail our car payment in. She

did so, but unfortunately, neglected to follow-up
and make sure that it had indeed, been received by Tyndall in
a timely manner.

In monitoring our checking account (where the payment
originated from), she realized that the check had not
been cleared in a timely manner and immediately made the
payment in person.

As we realize that this oversight was absolutely avoidable we
have implemented several measures to assure
that it never happens again. Not only do we make all payments
on all accounts either in person or online – as
that way, we know that the payment was received and credited
to the appropriate account, we also pay well
before the actual due dates.

In addition, we have implemented an easy-to-access ledger
system – both as a hard-copy physical ledger
book and an online tracking system. Both of which are
compared against each other and items paid and
"cleared" notated as such on at least a weekly basis.

3. Late payments dated 12/07 (and previous) in regards to
current ACME Student Loan –
current balance $23,132

In February 2000, we consolidated my student loans into one
loan payment with XXX, with the terms being
8% interest @ $242/month on a "Level Payment Plan." That
payment was more than manageable and we had
absolutely no issues in paying it.

In approximately 2002, our loan was "sold" to another lender
and our obligation immediately increased to
$504/month, despite being on the "Level Payment Plan."
When we called to inquire as to the circumstances
to this change, we were told that we "had always paid this
much" despite having payment coupon books and

a loan agreement to the contrary. Daunted, and not knowing our rights as per the Higher Education Act, we struggled to make those payments. My wife sought extra employment and I remained a Reservist in the Army National Guard simply to struggle to make the payments. As our income at that time was approximately $45,000/year combined and our housing costs (which were very reasonable for the area outside Washington, D.C) were $700/month, it was a losing battle.

Later that year, I accepted a position with the Federal Government for the job stability and higher income. While I was being paid more monthly, we still had such a large amount in arrears that it was almost impossible to catch up. While my income had increased, our housing costs had nearly doubled as well, making it difficult to become current in a timely fashion. All the while, the interest compounded and compounded, of course.

Approximately a year and a half ago, my father, who passed away after a long devastating illness, kindly left me a modest sum of money (approximately $10,000 after taxes). After the funds were "freed" from the estate, in April of this year, I used the majority of that money to become current with that account, while the rest went to purchase a solid, used, easy-to-maintain vehicle (rather than obtain another loan for a new purchase). Since that period of time, I have made on-time payments on this loan – paying slightly more than what is due and making the payments well before the due date.

Please note that from the time the issues began in 2002 until 06/2008, I repeatedly called ACME, asking for direction and explanations of the circumstances. On approximately 12 occasions over that time period, I asked for a copy of my promissory note and/or payment history (as they would not accept my hard copies of our transactions). Each time I was told it would be forthcoming. Each time, it was NOT.

In April, after I made the large payment bringing the account current, I stumbled upon a website called "MyFico Forums," a forum provided to the general public by the creators of the FICO Scoring System. It was there, after asking for advice on dealing with the matter of the exploded payment, that I was directed to call the Department of Education's office and inquire about the legalities of what I was dealing with. I was advised by a Resolution Specialist at the Department of Education that there was indeed an error on ACS's part and was advised to immediately request an audit/investigation from the Ombudsman's Office.

At this point in time (06/08), I was more concerned about my immediate credit scoring situation, and mindful of how long an investigation takes, I instead approached ACME's Resolution Team with the Department of Education's assessment and recommendation, asking for a resolution and credit reporting adjustment in accordance with their findings.

In 07/08, I was notified that there had, indeed, been a problem with our account and that they were unable to discover what had caused it (guesstimating that the "problem" occurred when the lender sold our account).
They were able to provide me with an (incorrect) copy of my promissory note – which I accepted – as I did request the loan and I have benefited from the education the loan is for. And lowered my payments from $504/month to $199/month, which I gladly accepted. Further, they agreed that because of the problems with the account, they would remove nearly a year's worth of lates.

I honestly cannot stress how difficult this entire situation has been and I apologize for the convoluted explanation – but it is how it occurred. I realize that most would have gone further and ordered a full investigation or prompted a lawsuit, but in the end, after dealing with this situation for over 6 years, we simply wanted it settled. Six years was more than enough.

4. Medical Collection – ACME Collection Agency 07/05 – $196 paid

This medical bill was the result of a medical emergency in 06/07. We never received a bill for these services and assumed (incorrectly) that our medical insurance paid the entire bill. Once we realized, via a phone call from a West Asset Management collection agent, that it had not been paid, we immediately paid this bill.

5. Medical Collection $56 due – unpaid

We have requested full debt validation from this collection agency and have never received a response from them. The little information given to us leads us to (firmly) believe it is NOT our bill, as the medical professional originating the account is not a provider any member of our family has ever seen.

We are still in the process of disputing this account as, again, we do not believe it is accurate.

6. Multiple Credit Card Inquiries

While our past credit is damaged horribly by the situation with the student loan servicer, ACS, at this point, we are able to move forward – and make our own future and better our credit files with solid payment history and new lines of responsibly used credit lines. To this end, we acquired a reasonable number of credit cards to begin rebuilding our credit, as recommended by FICO advisors and experts.

7. Four "New" Credit Card Accounts

As I mentioned before, I am doing my best to rebuild my credit-standing. To this end, I have applied and been approved for 3 major credit cards and 1 "store" card. In order to not incur more debt than I can reasonably pay off, I limit my usage of these accounts to what I can afford. However, as they are still relatively new, the fine "art" of using these cards and paying them before they report high balances to the Credit Bureaus is still one that I am learning. My balances are still, I believe, reasonable and fairly average.

We make a point of paying far, far, far more than the "minimum payment" on each one – and in fact, make multiple payments (which has been suggested to us by several FICO Forum experts) during the month.

In conclusion

While I admit that we have many issues that have affected our past credit-standing, we have implemented many measures to assure that our credit scores and worthiness will increase. While we have the luxury of a stable government job in this economy at an important base in the US Navy hierarchy, we also make a point of taking costsaving measures where we can. We have since cut back on luxury items such as cell phone bills, cable, entertainment expenses, and monitor our accounts and budget to the penny.

And please let me add that we completely understand the impact of a mortgage and the responsibility that goes with such a commitment. We have never, in the 11 years that we have rented our home, been late on a rental payment. While we see daily the effects of the current economy and can certainly understand a lender's aversion to the hint of "risk," we do believe that my stable job with the Federal Government, our rental history and the dedication we've shown to fixing our past mistakes and repairing our credit make us an excellent risk. We have weathered quite a bit of adversity, both personally and in regards to credit, and we have emerged stronger, wiser and more dedicated to doing what's "right" - not what's "easy."

Thank you very much for your time and consideration.

Very respectfully,
Mr. Wonderin

These samples can be found at:
http://ficoforums.myfico.com/t5/Mortgage-Loans/Letter-of-Explanation-sample/td-p/410563 and
http://www.repaircredit123.com/credit-repair-letters/

Collection
1. Request for Validation of Overdue
2. Debt Collection Agency Dispute

Sample 1: Request for Validation of Overdue

To Whom It May Concern:
I am writing this letter in response to the phone call/letter received from you on (Date). In conformance to my rights under the Fair Debt Collection Practices Act (FDCPA), I am requesting you to provide me with a validation of the debt that you talked of earlier. Please note, this a not a refusal to pay, rather a statement that your claim is disputed and validation is demanded. (15 USC 1692g Sec. 809 (b))
I do hereby request that your office provide me with complete documentation to verify that I owe the said debt and have any legal obligation to pay you.
Please provide me with the following:
1. Agreement with the creditor that authorizes you to collect on this alleged debt

2. The agreement bearing my signature stating that I have agreed to assume the debt

3. Valid copies of the debt agreement stating the amount of the debt and interest charges

4. Proof that the Statute of Limitations has not expired

5. Complete payment history on this account along with an accounting of all additional charges being assessed

6. Show me that you are licensed to collect in my state; and

7. Your license numbers and Registered Agent

If your office fails to reply to this debt validation letter within 30 days from the date of your receipt, all instances related to this account must be immediately deleted and completely removed from my credit file. Moreover, all future attempts to collect on the said debt must be ceased.

Your non-compliance with my request will also be construed as an absolute waiver of all claims to enforce the debt against me and your implied agreement to compensate me for court costs and attorney fees if I am forced to bring this matter before a judge.

Thanking you,

Your Signature_____

Your Name_____   _____

Sample 2: Debt Collection Agency Dispute

Initial Debt Collection Dispute Letter

Today's Date

Your Name

Your Address

Collector's Name

Collector's Address

Dear {insert name of collector or company},

I am writing in response to your (letter or phone call) dated {insert date}, (copy enclosed) because I do not believe I owe what you say I owe.

This is the first I've heard from you, or any other company on this matter therefore, in accordance with the Fair Debt Collection Practices Act, Section 809(b): Validating Debts: (b) If the consumer notifies the debt collector in writing within the thirty-day period described in subsection (a) that the debt, or any portion thereof, is disputed, or that the consumer requests the name and address of the original creditor, the debt collector shall cease collection of the debt, or any disputed portion thereof, until the debt collector obtains verification of the debt or any copy of a judgment, or the name and address of the original creditor, and a copy of such verification or judgment, or name and address of the original creditor, is mailed to the consumer by the debt collector.

I respectfully request that you provide me with the following information:

* (1) the amount of the debt;

* (2) the name of the creditor to whom the debt is owed;

* (3) Provide a verification or copy of any judgment (if applicable);

* (4) Proof that you are licensed to collect debts in (insert name of your state)

Be advised that I am fully aware of my rights under the Fair Debt Collection Practices Act and the Fair Credit Reporting Act. For instance, I know that:

* because I have disputed this debt in writing within 30 days of receipt of your dunning notice, you must obtain verification of the debt or a copy of the judgment against me and mail these items to me at your expense;

* you cannot add interest or fees except those allowed by the original contract or state law.

* you do not have to respond to this dispute but if you do, any attempt to collect this debt without validating it, violates the FDCPA;

Also be advised that I am keeping very accurate records of all correspondence from you and your company including recording all phone calls and I will not hesitate to report violations of the law to my State Attorney General, the Federal Trade Commission and the Better Business Bureau.

I have disputed this debt; therefore, until validated you know your information concerning this debt is inaccurate. Thus, if you have already reported this debt to any credit-reporting agency (CRA) or Credit Bureau (CB) then, you must immediately inform them of my dispute with this debt. Reporting information that you know to be inaccurate or failing to report information correctly violates the Fair Credit Reporting Act

1681s-2. Should you pursue a judgment without validating this debt, I will inform the judge and request the case be dismissed based on your failure to comply with the FDCPA.

Finally, if you do not own this debt, I demand that you immediately send a copy of this dispute letter to the original creditor so they are also aware of my dispute with this debt.

Signature here

Your Printed Name

These samples can be found at:
https://www.ovlg.com/letters/debt-validation-letter.html and http://consumerist.com/2007/07/18/sample-letter-for-disputing-a-debt-collection-notice/

Inquiry
1. Request for Credit Report Upon Denial
2. Unauthorized Inquiry Dispute

Sample 1: Request for Credit Report Upon Denial

Date:_____

Re: Request for Credit Report

To Whom It May Concern:

I have recently been denied credit as a result of information contained on my credit report. Enclosed is a copy of that credit denial. Please send a copy of my credit report to me at my current address:

_____

_____

_____

My social security number is _____. My birth date is _____. My current employer is _____. My previous employer was _____. I have lived at my current address for _____ years. My previous addresses during the last five years: _____. My spouse's name is _____.

Yours truly,

_____

- See more at: http://consumer.findlaw.com/credit-banking-finance/sample-request-for-credit-report-if-you-have-recently-been-denied.html#sthash.IPglLoLp.dpuf

Sample 2: Unauthorized Inquiry Dispute

[Your Name]

[Your Address]

[City, State Zip]

[DATE]

[Name of Company that did the inquiry]

[Their Address]

[City State Zip]

RE: Unauthorized Credit Inquiry

Dear: [Company Name],

I recently received a copy of my Credit Bureau Name credit report. The credit report showed a credit inquiry by your company that I do not recall authorizing. I understand that you shouldn't be allowed to put an inquiry on my file unless I have authorized it. Please have this inquiry removed from my credit file because it is making it very difficult for me to acquire credit. I have sent this letter certified mail because I need your prompt response to this issue.

Please be so kind as to forward me documentation that you have had the unauthorized inquiry removed. If you find that I am remiss, and you did have my authorization to inquire into my credit report, then please send me proof of this.

Thank you for your help,

[Your Signature]

_____

[Your name typed]

Bankruptcy

1. Letter of Explanation for Bankruptcy
2. Bankruptcy Beyond Statute of Limitation Dispute

Sample 1: Letter of Explanation for Bankruptcy

Dear Sir or Madam,

In response to your letter regarding the reasons for my bankruptcy from which I was discharged 18 months ago, this is in regard to my recent application for a loan with your company.

Back in 2002, I suddenly found myself out of a job when the company for whom I'd been working for as a Finance Manager for 10 years, were forced to go into liquidation. All of the workforce, including myself, were given no notice that this event was about to happen and as a result of finding myself suddenly out of work and aged 42, I found it difficult to find any alternative employment which was able to offer the same high level of income I had, up until that point, been accustomed to. With a mortgage, personal loan and other financial commitments to fulfill, I was thrust into a situation whereby I was unable to meet my considerable financial obligations which escalated over the subsequent months until the point where one of my creditors issued bankruptcy proceedings against me.

Since being discharged from bankruptcy, I have obtained another senior position within the financial sector, earning a good income with a company whose reputation is solid and whose prospects appear to be one of the most stable in the financial sector. Therefore, due to the mitigating circumstances surrounding my bankruptcy and the fact that I had no control over that alongside the fact that, up until that point, I had held down a well-paid, steady job for 10 years with the same company and have now obtained another secure position, I hope that this will explain the reasons for my bankruptcy and that you will be prepared to look favorably upon my application for a loan.

I have also included supporting documents of evidence to back up the explanation contained within this letter and if you require any further clarification or information, please do not hesitate to get in touch.

Yours faithfully,

Mr. Brian Swann

Sample 2: Bankruptcy Beyond Statute of Limitation Dispute Letter

Your Address
Goes Here

Data Control Officer
This Creditor
Data Controller Address

Dear Sirs

Re: Account Number xxxxxxxxxxx

After consultation with both the Information Commissioner
and the Credit Reference Agencies, I am writing directly to you
to request that you formally update my credit files in
accordance with the Data Protection Act.

I was declared bankrupt on <Date of your bankruptcy>and
subsequently discharged on <Date of Discharge>, and <name
of creditor> was included within the Bankruptcy. For your
convenience I have attached both my bankruptcy Order and
Discharge Notification.

Currently the information that you have recorded against my
name with the Credit Reference Agencies is factually
incorrect, and despite several written requests to your
customer services , as yet your company has failed to correct
the entries as required.

• It is requested that if you intend to default the account, the
default entry must be <Date if your bankruptcy>, in
accordance with the Data Protection Act.

• It is requested that you mark the account in some way as to
indicate that it is settled or satisfied, in accordance with the
Data Protection Act.

• If you have sold the debt on, according to the Information Commissioner, you are still liable to ensure that both you and the new holder are aware and that as the originator of the information it is your responsibility to ensure that it is corrected.

The Information Commissioner has indicated that I should allow you 28 calendar days from the date you receive this letter to comply, during this time you are requested either to update the Credit Reference Files correctly (of all three Credit Reference Agencies) or notify me in writing the reasons that you refuse to.

After the 28 days have elapsed the Information Commissioner has requested that I inform them if your company fails to update the records so that they may take any necessary enforcement action against your company.

I have copied the relevant information provided by the Information Commissioner as an attachment to this request.

Yours faithfully

Fred Bloggs

Enc:

Bankruptcy Order
Discharge Notification

This sample can be found at:
https://www.payplan.com/debt_questions/debt_forum/viewtopic.php?t=9431 **and** http://www.letterexpert.co.uk/letter-explaining-reasons-for-bankruptcy.html

Conclusion

Credit repair is almost a necessary endeavor to improve your financial well-being. Due to the recent economic crisis, applications for loans have never been more closely scrutinized. Aside from the buffer that credit can offer, loans can also be used to start businesses and fund investments. These steps towards financial freedom can be difficult without the right credit score.

Increasing your credit score and removing negative records cannot be done overnight. Most of the steps are easier said than done for other individuals struggling with the timely payments of debts. Although payment history has the heaviest weight in your overall financial score and has the greatest potential in repairing your credit reputation, it is not the only solution.

Debt utilization ratio, diversity of your credit portfolio and age of your accounts are some of the sure ways to repair your credit. Other creative ways are also available such as negotiations, goodwill adjustments and other exceptional but legal ways of repairing your score.

Aside from that, credit repair may be something that can be outsourced to a credit repair service agency. If you do not have the patience or the expertise to do it yourself, then you can always hire an agency to do it for you.

In the end, the goal of the repair and transformation is to make it as close as possible to reflecting your true financial performance. The report and score are meant to provide you access to the finances that you can safely and properly manage.

www.ingramcontent.com/pod-product-compliance
Lightning Source LLC
Chambersburg PA
CBHW070959180526
45168CB00003B/1210